INTRO TO
RODEO

BY MOLLY LAURYSSENS

SADDLE UP!

SportsZone

An Imprint of Abdo Publishing
abdopublishing.com

abdopublishing.com

Published by Abdo Publishing, a division of ABDO, PO Box 398166, Minneapolis, Minnesota 55439. Copyright © 2018 by Abdo Consulting Group, Inc. International copyrights reserved in all countries. No part of this book may be reproduced in any form without written permission from the publisher. SportsZone™ is a trademark and logo of Abdo Publishing.

Printed in the United States of America, North Mankato, Minnesota
092017
012018

Cover Photo: Juan Monino/iStockphoto
Interior Photos: Juan Monino/iStockphoto, 1; Scott Serio/ESW/Cal Sport Media/AP Images, 5; Tom Donoghue/Polaris/Newscom, 6; Haynes, St. Paul/Library of Congress, 8; Jason Connolly/AFP/Getty Images, 10–11; Luc Novovitch/Alamy, 12; Sue Ogrocki/ AP Images, 15, 17, 21, 22; Ed Blochowiak/Shawnee News-Star/AP Images, 18; Christian Petersen/Getty Images Sport/Getty Images, 24–25; Hugh Carey/Wyoming Tribune-Eagle/ AP Images, 27; Larry MacDougal/AP Images, 28–29; Brandy Taylor/iStockphoto, 30–31; iStockphoto, 33, 36–37, 39, 44–45; Uwe Anspach/EPA/Newscom, 35; DG Photography/ iStockphoto, 40; Michael Silver Travel/Alamy, 43

Editor: Marie Pearson
Series Designer: Laura Polzin
Content Consultant: Paige Clark, B.S. Equine Science, University of Minnesota Crookston

Publisher's Cataloging-in-Publication Data
Names: Lauryssens, Molly, author.
Title: Intro to rodeo / by Molly Lauryssens.
Description: Minneapolis, Minnesota : Abdo Publishing, 2018. | Series: Saddle up! | Includes online resources and index.
Identifiers: LCCN 2017946879 | ISBN 9781532113437 (lib.bdg.) | ISBN 9781532152313 (ebook)
Subjects: LCSH: Rodeos--Juvenile literature. | Horsemanship--Juvenile literature. | Horse sports--Juvenile literature.
Classification: DDC 791.84--dc23
LC record available at https://lccn.loc.gov/2017946879

TABLE OF
CONTENTS

CHAPTER 1
A DANGEROUS EIGHT SECONDS 4

CHAPTER 2
JUST FOR KICKS 14

CHAPTER 3
TIMING IS EVERYTHING 20

CHAPTER 4
WORKING COWS 34

GLOSSARY 46
ONLINE RESOURCES 47
MORE INFORMATION 47
INDEX 48
ABOUT THE AUTHOR 48

A DANGEROUS EIGHT SECONDS

Professional bull rider J. B. Mauney sits atop a big brown bull named Bruiser. Mauney is competing for the Professional Bull Riding (PBR) World Championship. Mauney grabs hold of a flat-braided rope, which is wrapped around Bruiser's chest behind his front legs. This grasp is one of the only things that will help Mauney stay on the bull—that, and a lot of courage and concentration.

Mauney nods his head and the chute opens. Bruiser leaps and spins into the arena. Mauney's free hand is not allowed to touch the bull. He holds it high in the air

This was not the first time Mauney had challenged Bruiser. The two had met previously in 2014.

as Bruiser bucks, jerks, and twists, attempting to throw Mauney to the ground.

Mauney needs to stay on Bruiser for a total of eight seconds for the victory. It's not a lot of time, but when a bull that weighs as much as 2,000 pounds (907 kg) is trying to throw him, it's quite an accomplishment. The crowd cheers as Mauney hangs on until those eight seconds are through. He has won the 2015 PBR World Championship. Bruiser, a prized athlete himself, would go on to win the 2016 PBR World Championship Bull title.

THE HISTORY OF RODEO

A rodeo is an exciting competition among cowboys and cowgirls to show off their riding talents and roping skills. *Rodeo* is a Spanish word meaning "roundup." The rodeo is believed to have started in Deer Trail, Colorado, in 1869, when two groups of cowboys from neighboring ranches got together to settle an argument. They wanted to compete to see who was better at their job.

Mauney hoists the 2015 PBR World Championship trophy.

In the 1860s, there were many cowboys and cowgirls who worked in ranches across the United States. Ranch hands were responsible for taking care of all the livestock on a ranch. Their work was both physically and mentally demanding. From horseback, they would often have to surround and round up livestock for medical treatments or for sale. Cowboys would often use a special rope, known as a lasso, to catch stray animals. They would also break, or tame, wild horses so they could be ridden.

RODEO TODAY

These types of tasks ultimately gave birth to the rodeo. Rodeos can be held inside a stadium or out in the open. They take place in a fenced-in, dirt-surfaced area known

Breaking a horse often meant riding it until the horse no longer resisted the rider on its back.

as an arena. While arena sizes vary, they all contain bucking and roping chutes. These are holding pens where animals are safely contained while they await competition. Although bull riding was never in a cowboy's job description, this sport emerged from the tough and fearless cowboy mentality. It has become a popular rodeo event.

Many organizations host rodeos, including the National High School Rodeo Association (NHSRA), Women's Professional Rodeo, and PBR. In all venues, sportsmanship, showmanship, and mentorship are important principles for successful competition. Each December, the Professional Rodeo Cowboys Association (PRCA) hosts the

The rodeo chute opens into the arena.

Wrangler Nationals Final Rodeo (NFR). It has been called the Super Bowl of rodeo. It is a competition that brings the top 15 athletes together at the end of the season to determine who is the best at the seven standard rodeo events: bareback bronc riding, saddle bronc riding, team roping, tie-down roping, bull riding, barrel racing, and steer wrestling.

In the past, some rodeo events only allowed males or females to compete, but recently events have become more open to all competitors. Competitors at all events can win prizes. The prizes can include money, belt buckles, livestock, saddles, and cars.

Women can compete in bull riding at some rodeos.

JUST FOR KICKS

The most popular and jaw-dropping feats to watch at a rodeo are referred to as rough stock events. Each of these events pits one rider against a bull or horse that might be more than five times the competitor's weight. There are three events that fall under this category: bull riding, saddle bronc riding, and bareback bronc riding.

The rider's score in these events is also dependent on the animal's performance. Typically, two judges rate both the animal and the rider, giving a score between 0 and 25 for a total of 100 possible points. The more a bull or horse

bucks and twists, the higher their potential score, which bodes well for the rider. The rider is scored on how well he stays balanced on the animal. Rodeo animals are prized and appreciated livestock and are considered just as much athletes as human competitors.

HORSEPLAY

Saddle bronc riding and bareback bronc riding are similar to bull riding. Riders must stay on a bucking horse for at least eight seconds while hanging on with only one hand.

JARED ALLEN'S BULLS

NFL player Jared Allen owns several PBR bulls. His bull Air Time bucked off every rider that challenged it in 2015 and 2016.

The main difference from bull riding is that with bareback and saddle bronc riding, the rider must "mark out" the horse. This means that the rider's spurs—metal tools that are attached to a rider's boots and used to give signals to a horse—must be touching the horse's shoulders as the pair leaves the chute. The spurs must remain on the horse's shoulders until the horse's hooves hit the ground. This encourages the horse to buck.

The ride in bareback bronc riding is the most physically demanding of the rough stock sports.

Different rodeo organizations have rules about spurs to make sure the horses do not get hurt. Spurs used in the PRCA must be dull and rounded so they cannot break the horse's skin, which is much thicker than human skin.

Saddle bronc riding and bareback riding also differ from each other. In bareback riding, as in bull riding, a leather strap is used to tie in a rider's hand and is the only thing keeping the rider on the horse. Bareback riding puts

more stress on a rider's body than any other rodeo event. This is because of how quickly and forcefully a horse can move and how little equipment keeps a rider on the horse's back.

Saddle bronc riding came from breaking horses for ranch work in the Old West. The rider holds on to a thick rein attached to the horse's halter. The rider also tries to remain seated in the saddle and must keep his feet in the stirrups, or else he is disqualified.

Horses used for bareback and saddle bronc riding are natural buckers. Some of these horses, including High Chaparral, kept bucking off trainers and owners. Others come from lines of horses bred to naturally buck. A strap lined with soft material is tied loosely in front of the horse's back legs. Horses buck higher with this flank strap. Rodeo organizations including the PRCA have many rules that protect the safety of the animals competing. If an animal is not healthy and well cared for, it will not perform well.

A saddle bronc rider tries to ride the horse smoothly, while bareback riders may be thrown around more.

3

TIMING IS EVERYTHING

While some rodeo events are all about strength, others are about speed. Steer wrestling is a timed event, but it looks pretty rough. The purpose of this event is to wrestle a steer to the ground as quickly as possible. The rules for the event are simple. The steer always gets a head start. He is released into the arena, and two riders on horseback race after him. The rider on the left of the steer is the steer wrestler. He is also called the bulldog. The other is the hazer. The hazer travels along the steer's right side to keep it from straying too far from the bulldog.

The transition from horse to steer is key to success.

When the riders catch up with the steer, the two can be galloping up to 30 miles per hour (48 km/h). Then the bulldog slides off his horse, grabbing the steer's horns and wrestling the steer to the ground as fast as he can.

The bulldog's timing when leaving the horse and tackling the steer determines his success. He must lean out of the saddle and grab the steer's horns when he's directly above the animal. But he needs to stay partially in the saddle for just a moment longer, letting the horse carry his feet in front of the steer. This helps him quickly turn the steer's head, using the steer's forward motion to bring it to the ground. This saves the bulldog time and energy, as a

steer can weigh twice as much as him. The bulldog who can wrestle a steer to the ground the fastest wins.

ROPING SKILLS

While cowboys in the past sometimes needed to handle livestock with their bare hands, they often had an important tool to help them out. A cowboy who could use a lasso while on horseback could catch an animal quickly. Roping events at the rodeo reflect these skills.

Team roping involves a team strategy. Two riders work together on horseback. Their goal is to tie a steer as fast as possible so he can't move. The steer gets a head start out of the chute. As the steer runs, one of the riders, known

In team roping, the steer wears horn wrapping to protect him from the rope.

as the header, first has to rope the steer's horns, one horn and head, or neck. The header has to be precise with his or her throw, making a perfect shot. The header turns the steer's hind legs toward the second rider, known as the

heeler. The heeler then ropes both rear feet. If the heeler
only catches one rear foot, seconds are added to their
time. The clock stops for this event when both horses face
each other in the arena and the ropes are tight.

TIE-DOWN ROPING

As in team roping, the goal in tie-down roping is to immobilize a calf. But one competitor must do it using only his horse and rope, which is attached to the horse's saddle. The calf receives a head start out of the chute. Then the competitor ropes him as quickly as possible while dismounting from the horse. The horse has to come to a complete stop.

After dismounting, the competitor races on foot to the calf. The horse is trained to pull away from the calf so that the rope is tight. The horse does not pull hard enough to drag the calf. The competitor then flanks the calf, flipping it onto the ground. He ties three legs together with a rope he has clenched in his teeth, known as a pigging string. The competitor then raises his hands to show the job is done.

The competitor gets back on his horse and rides forward to create slack in the rope to confirm that the calf hasn't moved. If the calf doesn't move in six seconds, then

Riders dismount as their horses are sliding to a stop.

the competitor has done his job well. But if the calf breaks the tie, the ride does not qualify.

A similar event to tie-down roping is breakaway roping. Breakaway roping simply demonstrates a competitor's ability to throw a lasso around a calf's neck while on horseback. Once the calf is roped, the rider stops his or her horse to tighten the rope. The rope is tied to the saddle with a string. When the string breaks as the calf pulls, the rope falls. That is when time is called.

WEAVING AND CIRCLING

Pole bending is a timed event. Poles are arranged in a straight line. The horse and rider weave in and out of

Competitors reach for three of the calf's legs before it is on the ground.

them as quickly as possible. If a pole gets knocked over during the ride, there is a five-second penalty added to the rider's score. The fastest time wins. Fast times for pole bending are around 20 seconds.

Much like pole bending, barrel racing is a timed event where a mounted rider and horse move as swiftly as possible. Barrel racing originally started as a women's sport. These days anyone can compete in some venues. Some people race for fun, while others compete professionally. Three 55-pound (25-kg) barrels are arranged in a triangle. The horse and rider cross the timer line to start the clock. Then they circle each barrel in

In pole bending, weaving too wide can cost time, while weaving too tight can knock a pole down.

a cloverleaf pattern, starting with either the left or right barrel. From there, they then circle the opposite barrel, run around the top barrel, and race as fast as they can back across the timer line. If they knock a barrel over, they lose seconds off their time. If the barrel racer doesn't follow the correct pattern, he or she is disqualified. The rider with the fastest time wins. Barrel racing takes grace as well as good communication between the horse and rider.

MAKING A NAME

In November 2016, Chayni Chamberlain became the youngest athlete to compete in the Elite Rodeo Association's The American rodeo. At 11 years old, she beat many top barrel racers in the semifinals on her horse Flo. She did not win the finals, but she earned many fans and continues to shine in the arena.

BARREL
RACING GEAR

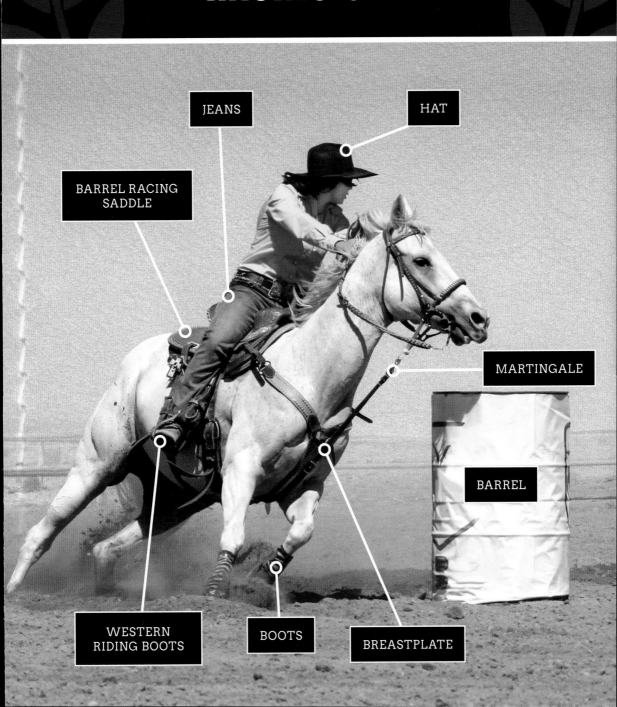

JEANS

HAT

BARREL RACING SADDLE

MARTINGALE

BARREL

WESTERN RIDING BOOTS

BOOTS

BREASTPLATE

4

WORKING COWS

Some rodeo events aren't timed at all but are judged. The reined cow horse event is one. It takes place on horseback and requires skillful handling and communication between horse and rider. The reined cow horse event highlights the control a horse can exert over a cow, which was necessary during cattle drives where the number of cattle could run into the hundreds.

The horse and rider are evaluated in skills horses need to manage cattle. The horse must show it can come to a quick, sliding stop. It should back up and do lead changes,

In the sliding stop, a horse leans back on its rear legs to quickly stop.

which means changing the leg a horse is leading with at the lope. The team is also judged on the horse's ability to keep a cow at one end of an arena for a certain amount of time. This is called boxing. The pair must then run the cow in a line and make it turn along the fence. Finally, the horse and rider must make the cow turn in a full circle in both directions without the help of a fence. They must control the cow the whole time.

Riders can get up to 80 points each for the reining phase and the cow phase. They lose points for not performing the reining pattern correctly or if the horse misbehaves. An average score is 70 points.

In reined cow horse, the rider cuts off the cow as it runs along the fence, forcing it to turn around.

Cutting horse is similar to reined cow horse in that a horse has to control the movements of a cow. In cutting horse, the horse enters a herd of cattle and must separate one cow from the herd. The team is allowed two and a half minutes to work, and judges can award anywhere from 60 to 80 points. The horse is judged on factors such as whether it enters the herd of cattle and brings one out with little or no disruption to the animals. A well-ridden event gives the impression that the horse and rider are reading the cow's mind. They anticipate the cow's movements and cut it off before it takes off.

OTHER RODEO COMPETITIONS

Rodeos aren't just about horses and cattle. Goat tying is typically seen at junior, college, and high school rodeo events. This event is gaining popularity. The point of this sport is to contain the goat quickly. It is similar to tie-down roping, except the goat starts off tied with a 10-foot (3.1-m) rope to a stake. The horse and rider race from the start line to the goat. The rider dismounts and

A cutting horse needs to keep the cow from rejoining the herd.

flips the goat onto its side, tying three of its legs together. Whoever ties the goat the quickest wins.

Since 2007 the NHSRA has offered shooting events for both junior and high school divisions. These consist of rifle competitions and trap shootings, in which contestants shoot targets that are in midair. Contestants shoot at targets 50 yards (45.7 m) away. The top four from the state can compete at the National Finals.

The NHSRA queen contest is for girls of each state and province in the National High School Rodeo Association. It is similar to other beauty pageants, but girls are also tested on the NHSRA rules and are judged for their horsemanship. For the horsemanship phase, they follow a set pattern of movements, including a walk, trot, lope,

SHOOTING EVENTS

Contestants must shoot 12 targets each while standing, kneeling, and lying on their stomachs facing the target. They are scored on how close to the center of the target their shots land.

Goat tying competitors must securely tie three legs as quickly as possible.

sliding stop, and circles. There is also a PRCA Miss Rodeo America contest each year. The winner is selected at the NFR event in December each year. She travels throughout the country and promotes the various rodeo events.

TRAINING FOR RODEO

Each event takes a lot of training and practice. Riders need to learn how to complete their event smoothly and quickly so they can get the fastest time. Riders who are interested in competing in an event should find a good trainer. Trainers give helpful tips for how to improve a horse and rider's performance.

Any horse can successfully compete in rodeo events. The most widely used breed in rodeo is the American quarter horse. It is popular because it often remains calm around livestock, but it is also able to move quickly. Paints and Appaloosas are also common. Whatever the horse's lineage, training is key to success. It must get used to the distractions of competition, such as lights and cheering crowds, as well as livestock. Regular exercise and a good diet enable horses to perform their best.

Miss Rodeo Texas opens a rodeo in 2015.

Some skills rodeo horses need to learn include starting in a box. The box is where a horse and rider wait while a steer gets a head start. Horses may also need to know how to perform a sliding stop. This is when a horse is moving

at a high speed and then quickly shifts its weight to its back legs, sliding to a halt. Horses in tie-down roping need to know to stop when their riders dismount. They then need to know to tighten any slack on the rope without dragging the calf.

A WILD RIDE

Rodeo is filled with many exciting, fast-paced events. Contestants need to be tough for the rough stock events. They need to have a good relationship with their horses for timed and judged events. Competitors and fans alike become addicted to this sport that keeps the Old West alive today.

The quarter horse is built for quick speed and sharp turns.

GLOSSARY

BOX
A gated area where a horse and rider wait to take off into the arena.

BREAK
To train a horse for riding or other things.

BRONC
An untrained horse.

BUCK
A movement where an animal kicks its feet in the air, trying to throw a rider.

BULL
A male cow.

CALF
A young cow.

CHUTE
A pen that holds an animal until it is opened and the animal is released into the arena.

DISMOUNT
To get off a horse's back.

HORSEMANSHIP
The skill of working with horses.

LASSO
A rope with a loop on one end that tightens around a caught animal when pulled.

LOPE
A horse's three-beat gait that is faster than a trot but slower than a gallop.

SPURS
Metal tools that are attached to a rider's boots and used to give signals to a horse.

STAKE
A post anchored in the ground.

STEER
A male cow or ox that has been surgically made unable to reproduce.

ONLINE RESOURCES

Booklinks
NONFICTION NETWORK
FREE! ONLINE NONFICTION RESOURCES

To learn more about rodeo, visit **abdobooklinks.com**. These links are routinely monitored and updated to provide the most current information available.

MORE INFORMATION

BOOKS

Clutton-Brock, Juliet. *Horse*. Relaunch ed. New York: DK Publishing, 2016.

Hamilton, John. *Rodeo Clown*. Minneapolis, MN: Abdo Publishing, 2016.

Hamilton, S. L. *Rodeo*. Minneapolis, MN: Abdo Publishing, 2010.

INDEX

Allen, Jared, 16

bareback bronc riding, 13, 14, 16–17, 19
barrel racing, 13, 31–32, 33
Bruiser, 4, 7
bucking, 10, 16, 19
bull riding, 4, 7, 9, 10, 13, 14, 16–17
bullfighters, 9

Chamberlain, Chayni, 32
cutting horse, 38

goat tying, 38–41

High Chaparral, 19
history, 7–9

Mauney, J. B., 4, 7

National High School Rodeo Association (NHSRA), 10, 41
NHSRA queen contest, 41

pole bending, 28, 31
PRCA Miss Rodeo America, 42
prizes, 13
Professional Bull Riding (PBR), 4, 7, 10, 16
Professional Rodeo Cowboys Association (PRCA), 10, 17, 19, 42

reined cow horse, 34, 37

saddle bronc riding, 13, 14, 16–17, 19
safety, 19, 24
shooting events, 41
steer wrestling, 13, 20–23

team roping, 13, 23–25
tie-down roping, 13, 26, 28, 38, 45
training, 42–43, 45

Women's Professional Rodeo, 10
Wrangler Nationals Final Rodeo (NFR), 13, 42

ABOUT THE AUTHOR

Molly Lauryssens is an award-winning sports reporter and freelance writer. She loves learning about the intricate details of athletes and the sports they play. She is a lover of any and all games.